# *Alyson Rodges'*
# PILLARS OF PACK LEADERSHIP®

Welcome to
The Pillars of Pack Leadership®

A practical guide to living life with your dog
in a safe, sane, and civilized way!

Alyson Rodges

The Pillars of Pack Leadership

A practical guide to living life with your dog
in a safe, sane, and civilized way!

Alyson Rodges

THE PILLARS OF PACK LEADERSHIP®
Alyson Rodges
First edition © 2017

All rights reserved.

This book or parts thereof may not be reproduced in any form, stored in a retrieval system, or transmitted in any form by any means—electronic, mechanical, photocopy, recording, or otherwise—without prior written permission of the publisher, except as provided by United States of America copyright law.

www.alysonrodges.com

ISBN-13: 978-1976336331

Printed in the United States

Dedicated to my family, my friends, my faith, and my dogs, who sustain me…

# OVERVIEW

The Pillars of Pack Leadership® is a behavioral approach to working with dogs that is rooted in more than mere commands—it's rooted in relationship. Our program focuses on understanding dogs' primal drives and instincts so humans can learn to "speak dog" and better communicate with them. Our entire training philosophy encourages your dog to live in a calm state of mind—what I call the concept of JUST BE, which develops the ability in your dog to make good choices. Helping your dog learn how to live life in a calm state of mind is truly the best thing I could ever teach you or your dog. Yes, *calm* is a decision. And yes, it's a skill that is taught. It's never too early or too late to begin this journey. The earlier you start, the better it is! Once the proper foundation is put into place, everything becomes much easier for you both.

It's not enough that I train your dog to do something for *me*. I have to be able to share that knowledge with you in practical ways that fit into your daily life—and that is my specialty. This guide breaks down my core training strategies into very manageable blocks of information that real people can implement. Whether you are a first-time or experienced dog owner, this guide is a big toolbox of the skills and knowledge necessary to successfully express calm, confident leadership within yourself and with your pack. You'll be "speaking dog" very soon. Remember, not every rule and guideline is forever!

# TABLE OF CONTENTS

| | |
|---|---|
| OVERVIEW | i |
| THE LINGO | v |
| THE FOUNDATION | 1 |
| THE FIVE PILLARS OF PACK LEADERSHIP | 13 |
|     ESTABLISHING EFFECTIVE STRUCTURE | 15 |
|     ESTABLISHING EFFECTIVE RITUALS | 27 |
|     MASTERING PURPOSE-DRIVEN ACTIVITIES | 33 |
|     ESTABLISHING RESPECT OF SPACE AND | |
|     CREATING SPACE BOUNDARIES | 46 |
|     MASTERING THE HUMAN PART OF THE EQUATION | 48 |
| COMMANDS | 56 |
| THE WHOLE DOG | 66 |
| CONCLUSION | 72 |
| ACKNOWLEDGMENTS | 74 |
| REFERENCES | 76 |

# THE LINGO

Dog-training terms can be pretty jargony. My goal is to make it clear and concise for the average dog owner and to ensure that we have a shared framework of understanding for our applications when using a term in our guide.

- LEADERSHIP: I've taken my definition of leadership from Jim Rohn, an author and motivational speaker: "The challenge of leadership is to be strong, but not rude; be kind, but not weak; be bold, but not bully; be thoughtful, but not lazy; be humble, but not timid; be proud, but not arrogant; have humor, but without folly."

- PURPOSE-DRIVEN ACTIVITY: When you are with your dog and ready to *focus* on, *interact* with, and *supervise* him, providing an outlet for his mental and physical energy. The activity has rules and specific objectives.

- APPROPRIATE CONFINEMENT: The action of confining or the state of being confined. For our purposes it applies to a crate, kennel, or exercise pen.

- DIRECT PRESSURE: Anything touching the dog directly (hands, leash, collar, etc.). Includes elements of molding.

- INDIRECT PRESSURE: Eye contact, tonal words/sounds, and body language applied to the dog with a gap of space—no physical contact—between the two parties (handler to dog or dog to dog). In handler-to-dog interactions, it includes elements of luring, shaping, and capturing.

- TIMING: The time you choose to work on a behavior or stop working on a behavior. The timing of a marker, reward, or correction. The timing of the application or release of direct or indirect pressure.

- PLACE: A defined space with a visual boundary, like a raised dog bed, blanket, or place board.

- YIELD: Using indirect pressure to move a dog into a lower body position. It's used as a way to tone down, slow down, or correct a behavior or mindset.

- FIGHT: A state of mind in which your dog can thrash his head around or paw at his leash or other training tool. The dog can make noise, bark, whine, growl, or bite. Dog can move backwards away from you, jump up, try to get away, come up the leash at you, bite his leash, freeze up and shake, lie down, or jump around and alligator roll. Fight might occur when you apply pressure in any new way.

- FLIGHT: A state of mind in which your dog can move away from you with intent to remove himself from a situation.

- AVOIDANCE: A state of mind in which your dog can keep away from you or refuse to obey a specific command or instruction. A dog can look the other direction, hold his head down, sit on human, lean on human, keep mouth closed, repeatedly lick lips, or yawn.

- ACCEPTANCE: A state of mind in which your dog's behavior is received as adequate or suitable. Your dog will look relaxed and comfortable, with soft eyes, a soft body, an open mouth, a smooth forehead, and soft ears.

# THE FOUNDATION:
## Good Stuff to Know Before You Begin

Your dog was born with a combination of strong tendencies that were inherited from his parents. Understanding what these are *before* any training begins will give you many insights into his personality, his natural temperament, and how he perceives the world. The truth is, average people have lives that need to be lived with work, family, and different obligations, so it sure helps to know the kind of dog you are inviting into your life. The breed and temperament of a dog you choose has consequences. Be prepared to live a life that supports the nature of the dog you choose.

Why is it so critical to know who your dog is by birth? The most important reason is that understanding inherited traits will help you understand the *individual* your dog is and what his strengths and weaknesses are. Once you can correctly identify the qualities in your dog, you can tailor your training strategies to best impact the mind and heart of your pooch! The good news is that no matter who your dog is by birth, with effective training tools and implementation of the Pillars of Pack Leadership, you can improve any dog's state of mind and his interaction with the world.

*Prey, Pack, and Defense Drives*

It is important to know that dogs have some combination of three drives: prey, pack, and defense. What varies is their intensity within each drive category. There are many books and articles out there on the subject, but I think that Jack and Wendy Volhard's "Canine Personality Profile" describes it in a clear and concise way for the average dog owner. Here is my "CliffsNotes" interpretation of their article:

Prey Drive: Behaviors inherited are associated with retrieving, hunting, killing, and eating prey. Prey-drive behaviors include scenting, tracking, talking, chasing, pouncing, high-pitched barking, jumping, biting, pulling down, tearing things apart, and carrying, digging, and burying objects.

Examples: Labrador or Border collie

Prey-drive motivators include the use of:
- motion (hand signals)
- enthusiastic tone (like a high-pitched tone)
- anything a dog will work for (like a treat or toy)

Pack Drive: Behaviors inherited are governed by a sense of rank order in the social hierarchy. Physical contact, playing, willingness to work as part of a team, and any behaviors associated with social interaction with others are dominant characteristics. Typical behaviors include licking ears, mounting, and other courting gestures. This type of dog enjoys social order and connection with his leader, so he might have a hard time being away from his owner for extended periods of time. This dog has great instincts for working with you and is great for a life filled with jobs to do with his human (living on a farm, going hiking, playing with kids, etc.).

Examples: Bernese mountain dog or labradoodle

Pack-drive motivators include the use of:
- physical affection and inviting body postures
- verbal praise and a friendly voice
- grooming
- smiling at the dog

Defense Drive: Behaviors inherited are governed by the instincts for survival and self-preservation and are comprised of both fight and flight behaviors. This natural drive can be elicited by a threatening body posture, direct eye contact, forward motion, hitting, and an unfriendly voice. Fight behaviors are characterized by a dog that "stands his ground" with ears and whiskers pointed forward and his tail held up. While standing tall, he stares at other dogs and likes to "strut his stuff." He will go toward unfamiliar objects or situations. He may guard his food, toys, or territory from other dogs or people. He will lie or sit in front of doorways or cupboards, making his owner walk around him. At the same time, he can tolerate a firmer hand; however, note that a threatening, harsh tone or hovering or leaning over or toward your dog may elicit a response you were not prepared for! Clear communication and firm, fair, and gentle handling are critical with all dogs, but for a dog with a strong defense drive—it's essential. (NOTE: There is an appropriate time to implement defensive strategies with all dogs. How much and how intense varies per dog.) These dogs can be a bit better at spending time alone and are great for guarding, protecting, or police work.

Examples: German shepherd

Defense-drive motivators include the use of:
· leaning over the dog
· checking on the leash (a sharp tug on the leash)
· using a harsh tone with the dog

Your dog already knows how to switch instantaneously from one drive to another. For example, Fido is playing with his favorite toy (prey), then the doorbell rings, and he drops the toy and starts to bark (defense). You open the door, and it's a friend Fido knows. Fido comes to greet your friend (pack) and returns to play with his toy (prey). Your dog will have a mixture, in varying degrees, of the prey, pack, and defense drives. Learning to apply correct strategies based upon who your dog is will help your dog learn to switch from prey drive to pack drive or from defense drive to pack drive upon your request. Better yet, he'll do it himself once he knows what you expect from him. What you do, how you do it, and how firmly you do it will depend on his current state of mind and where you want him to be instead.

*Real Life Example*: My personal pack is comprised of dogs with low prey drive, lower defense drive, and higher pack drive. These dogs are real charmers! They will follow me everywhere, don't get into much trouble, like to be with me, and are not that interested in chasing everything that moves. Not much distracts them, and not much ruffles them. They can figure out what I want and are easy to train and motivate. Mistakes on the human's part are not that critical. This type of dog really wants to find a calm state of mind, and once he does, you've got a balanced, compliant, accepting companion for life!

## *Beneficial Socialization*

If you have a pup or dog, you might have heard about how important it is to socialize your dog to other dogs and to different sights, sounds, textures, people, places, and things. The more the better, the sooner the better! We have a wonderful window of opportunity between the ages of eight to sixteen weeks to successfully expose a pup to all the world has to offer him. He is most receptive and willing to learn about his new world at this formative developmental stage. Socialization permanently shapes his future personality and how he will react to things in his environment as an adult. Done well, proper socialization and good training help a pup grow into a confident, relaxed, well-adjusted, accepting, pleasant dog that copes well, regardless of the situation.

A properly socialized and trained dog has the ability to make sound choices in the face of an unpredictable world. After training over 1,200 puppies and dogs, I can promise you, socialization is essential and the lack of it is detrimental, even life-threatening. Shelters, rescues, and training facilities are filled with dogs that are under-socialized and ill-prepared to navigate the intricacies of living in our human world where choices have consequences. In this quest to expose our dogs to many things, I add this to our journey: I say that merely exposing your pup or dog to stimuli isn't enough—you have to ensure that the exposure is actually beneficial to your dog. Listen, not every friend you've ever had in your life was necessarily a good influence. Not every exposure to a new thing in your life helped you or benefitted you. And finally, not every choice you made in life had delightful consequences. The same is true for our pups and dogs! It is so important to notice, understand, and correctly interpret how your dog perceives these new experiences and to help him understand what are acceptable and unacceptable choices to make while experiencing it.

Oh my, are you overwhelmed yet? Don't be. Just remember a few guiding principles as you go live life with your dog. Your dog takes his cues from you. Unexpected things happen in life, even unpleasant things. But we don't have to be defined by them forever, and neither does your dog. Here's the bottom line about all the fears, insecurities, surprises, accidents, all the noises and things that go bump in the night: The answer is always *calm, confident leadership* filled with a life of structure, boundaries, purpose-driven exercise, and earned affection. Don't get ruffled. Don't get frazzled. Get your emotion out of it so your dog can get over it. Finally, a good rule of thumb is not to put or leave your dog in a situation that you wouldn't think is safe, sane, healthy, and wise for a child.

### *Four States of Mind*

In your quest to establish a calm state of mind in your dog, you will find that your pooch will vacillate between four stages at one point or another. At any given moment, your dog will be in a state of:

1. Fight
2. Flight
3. Avoidance
4. Acceptance (notice I didn't merely say *compliance*, more on that later)

The goal is that you confidently move through stages 1-3 and get to stage 4. Believe it or not, with practice, patience, and perseverance, you get there more quickly and easily as you consistently work with your dog. And truthfully, as you learn how to be effective in your communication with your dog and set your pooch up for success, the fight won't be so dramatic, the flight desire will diminish, the level and duration of avoidance will be reduced, and you will achieve more than mere compliance to your request—you will actually be in the sweet spot called *acceptance*. At this point, you are building trust and a strong relationship with your dog. At this point, your dog will truly be able to embrace and enjoy a calm state of mind.

Often times, people react emotionally to the fight and flight states. They are not prepared for it and can react in ways that actually intensify the dog's fight-or-flight response. Some common reactions people have are: freezing up, trying to shove a treat into the dog's face, letting go of the leash, or stomping their feet and yelling "stop!" Basically, people get frustrated and sometimes panicky because they don't know what to do. The best protection against these inappropriate reactions is to prepare yourself for them by learning to recognize which state of mind your dog is in.

Dogs can be very creative in how they express fight and flight states. Some common things you'll see: dogs running away from you, thrashing their heads around, pawing at or biting their leash or training tools, making noise, moving backwards away from you, jumping up, trying to get away, coming up the leash at you, freezing up, rolling around like an alligator, and shaking. Just know that if you learn how to correctly stick with your training, these phases will pass. Don't weaken, don't stop, hold steady until the fight or flight moment is over. Then, RELAX. BREATHE. STOP. BREATHE.

Now that you know you will face flight/fight/avoidance moments (and it doesn't scare the heck out of you), you can continue to work with your dog until you reach Nirvana—the sweet spot of acceptance. And here is where it can get tricky. Just because the fight/flight moment is over doesn't necessarily mean you are at acceptance. Often times, there is this middle phase called *avoidance* and/or merely *compliance*. If you are not adept at reading a dog's body language, it is very easy to mistake avoidance and compliance for acceptance. Have you ever seen a dog sitting by his owner, but his head is turned away, lips are tight, mouth is shut, eyes are straining away, and ears are in a tight position? This dog is being compliant, but not accepting. If you misread avoidance and compliance for acceptance, you will have missed the most important part of the puzzle. And again, wait until you achieve it. WAIT. BREATHE. RELAX. Eventually, you'll get to acceptance.

So what is the real difference between acceptance and compliance? *Accept* means "to consent to receive something offered; the action or process of being received as adequate or suitable." On the other hand, *compliance* is defined as "the action or fact of complying with a wish or command." Concerning a dog-human relationship, I think the difference is significant. There are many ways to force or gain compliance with a dog, but it takes relationship, trust, and technique to gain acceptance.

And how do you know when you have acceptance? I wish I had an easy answer for you. It takes experience and practice to see it. It takes a genuine desire to learn how to "speak dog" better. It takes the time it takes for you to be able to recognize the signs that signal the move to a state of acceptance, such as a soft, opening mouth, a relaxed body, a soft eye, a smelling nose, ears in a soft, neutral position, and a soft, yielding body, just to name a few.

Once you've gotten to acceptance is the moment when all pressure—meaning leash pressure, spatial pressure, physical or voice pressure, etc.—needs to cease. If pressure remains too long, you can push a dog right back into the previous stages of fight, flight, and avoidance.

My goal in talking to you about these four stages of fight, flight, avoidance, and acceptance is to encourage you to become observers of dogs as you learn to live life in a new way with your pooch and to teach you how to recognize when you've actually reached the acceptance stage. So don't fret, don't fear, don't be afraid to fail on this journey. This process takes time. The reality here is that you just have to jump in and begin. It takes what it takes for you and your dog to work through these different stages. Prepare yourself, get your emotions out of the way, and get ready to work your way to acceptance.

### *JUST BE: A Calm State of Mind*

Good dog training should ultimately give you the skills you need so that you can absolutely influence the decisions of your dog upon a request or command, and your training should result in your dog being able to accept and execute those requests. However, *great* dog training is when you don't need to use those commands to be able to live life together.

I'm the youngest of five children and never had my own *anything*. It was hand-me-down everything until I got my first dog for my twelfth birthday. All I wanted to do was learn how to train my new girl, my very own Australian cattle dog. I begged my mom to let me take Kizzie to obedience classes. She finally gave in, and off I went. My dog bit the instructor on day one. Not a very auspicious beginning for this young, aspiring dog trainer. I was mortified; plus, the lady who was going to teach me everything I desperately wanted to know just got bit right in front of me. I was more determined than ever to figure this all out! I learned heel/sit/down/stay/come with the best of them and won the top award in that novice class.

And yet, even after all that, I still had a dog that had some strange, neurotic behaviors back at home. She would obsessively run the fence line or jump up and bounce against our windows when she was excited. I couldn't treat it, yell it, command it, ignore it, or startle it out of her. Kizzie just wouldn't stop, no matter what techniques I tried or classes I attended. Kizzie even ended up blind in one eye because I couldn't get her to come when she took off after my horse and was kicked in the face. All those commands and blue ribbons didn't work when real life distractions kicked in. They also didn't take into account her strong cattle dog prey drive. But at that time, I had no insight into those things, which certainly weren't prevalent ideas in the teachings I had access to. I knew something was missing, but it took years before I could put the pieces together.

And then came Izzie, my very first labradoodle. She came into my life and helped me understand the missing links I didn't know. My Izzie, the dog who stole my heart, was such a great communicator with other dogs and became the catalyst for my examination and understanding of dogs on a different level.

What I've discovered on this journey of learning how to "speak dog" is that the art of dog training is knowing when you've done *just enough*, *not enough*, or *more than enough*. If the perfect down/stay or militant-style compliance is your ultimate goal, then we have different goals. And if you've done all you know how to do—all the commands, praise, clickers, or treats—and your dog is *still* not where you want her to be on some issues, then you've discovered this truth that has become my driving, burning conviction that compels me in my relationships with dogs: **You can't command** *calm*, **and you can't compel** *acceptance!*

If we are commanding our dog every millisecond of the day, our dogs aren't thinking, growing, maturing, or deciding anything. You should be able to be with your dog, on or off a leash, out in society without compelling him into a command. You should not have to put a dog into a sit/down/stay position when a person approaches, just because he will jump on the person otherwise. I want my dog to be able to handle the excitement of an approaching person and *choose* to be polite and respectful. I'll even give my dog the option of choosing what makes him most comfortable in that situation, whether sitting, standing, lying down, or moving around a bit. I let him be aware of his world and aware of me. He is not sitting, glued onto the concrete with eyes glued to mine. He is learning how to relax and *choose* calm.

At Aly's Puppy Boot Camp (APBC), we expose our pups and dogs to other people of all ages, a variety of animals (dogs, cats, horses, goats, bunnies, chickens), and different sight sensations, smell sensations, texture sensations, noises, etc. Since life is often crazy, busy, noisy, smelly, and full of surprises, it is important that your pooch has the ability to maintain composure in the face of stimuli of all kinds. How your pup or dog is exposed to different stimuli is critical; the key—they must be *calmly* exposed! Once a dog can learn to think, make good choices, and handle all that life has to offer in a calm, safe, sane, and civilized way, then he is actually in the state of JUST BE. And truly, I believe that the greatest thing you can teach a dog is the art of JUST BE.

## Four Rules of JUST BE

I have four general principles about how dogs should be acting and the choices they should be making when hanging out around me, no matter what we are doing together. I want my dog to relax and know that as long as he doesn't break my four rules, it's all good and he has some leeway about what he can and can't do. These principles guide me in every facet of my working with a dog. The following should *never* happen:

#1: Dog, don't make me spill my scalding hot coffee, not even one drop.
#2: Dog, don't do anything to irritate me.
#3: Dog, don't do anything to irritate anyone or anything around me.
#4: Dog, don't do anything to piss me off.

If a dog breaks one of these four rules of JUST BE, I *shut down the silliness*, instantly and effectively. To shut down the silliness (meaning anything a dog is choosing other than what I'm asking for), it is imperative that you can hold your leash and quickly and firmly move your dog in a counter-clockwise motion back around to your side, then put him into a sit. As you are beginning to move your dog around in that "stirring a cauldron" motion, you take a step back simultaneously to aid in your arms momentum to get your dog around and back to your side as quickly as possible. Then immediately release the pressure of the leash the millisecond their butt hits the ground. Now, *just breathe*. Release ALL pressure and tension on the leash. Don't do anything. *Wait*. Let your dog decide if he is done choosing silliness. If he chooses to break a rule again, no problem, you just efficiently and quickly move that dog around to your side, get a sit, and release the pressure. Timing counts on this. How many times will a dog test you on whether or not you will shut down the silliness? It varies from dog to dog. Stick with this, and I promise, before very long your dog will decide that learning how to JUST BE is way more easy and gratifying than being silly.

That's it, gang. It really is. Yes, sits are nice, heels are fabulous, long-distance downs are exceptional, tricks are fun, tasks are helpful; but the ability to JUST BE—well, it's priceless.

# THE FIVE PILLARS OF PACK LEADERSHIP

My beloved Izzie taught me the missing links of information that I never learned from my obedience classes. As I watched her be her amazing self with other dogs, she taught me that dogs respond to order. They respect firm, fair, and compassionate leadership. Dogs respond to spatial and social nuances and do not tolerate uninvited infringements of space without a consequence. They mean what they say, and they don't have to be mean to mean it.

Essentially, mama dogs have been preparing their puppies for cohesive pack life since the beginning of time. They do this by giving them structure, boundaries, limitations, and affection (yes, in that order). A new pup was told when to eat and when to stop eating, when to sleep and when to wake up, when to come close or get away, when to stop doing something mama didn't like, when to play, and when to leave mom or her littermates alone. When we take a pup from his mama, this pup now joins a human pack. It's up to you whether you continue this balanced foundation, which was started by the mama and instilled by nature's wiring. It is very important that you implement strategies that help to establish and maintain healthy pack leadership in your home.

The Five Pillars of Pack Leadership teaches you these principles and helps establish you (human) as an effective leader in your partnership with your pooch. The five pillars we will discuss in detail include:

- Establishing Effective Structure
- Establishing Effective Rituals
- Mastering Purpose-Driven Activities
- Establishing Respect of Space and Creating Space Boundaries
- Mastering the Human Part of the Equation

These pillars help you establish and maintain your dog's calm state of mind in any situation, and most importantly, they are the vehicle to the changes we seek in our dogs so you can go live life together!

# Establishing Effective Structure

In order for your dog to be able to live life in a balanced way, you have to provide structure. What is structure? Structure is living life purposefully and intentionally with your dog. In the life of a dog, freedom needs to be earned. Dogs need jobs, and they need purpose. Getting along and learning how to JUST BE is how dogs live. That is how dogs become balanced. We set our pooches up for success by putting them in situations where we are prepared to follow through, guide them, mentor them, build relationship with them, and enable them to make good choices. It's never too late or too early to begin. All dogs, and even eight-week-old puppies, are naturally wired to accept this order, so let's get it right from the start, and we've got it right for life!

### *Crating and Appropriate Confinement*

To crate or not to crate, that is the question. The answer is simple: *Crate your pup or emotionally and behaviorally immature dog!* Crating is one component in the many strategies that you will use to bring balance and calm to your pooch. Crating is *far* more instrumental in your dog's state of mind than merely potty training. We use a crate daily in APBC's training programs because it uses a dog's natural den instincts and gives a dog a safe place to truly rest and relax. Dogs are not people, with our distaste for small, enclosed places. They are denning animals that, by choice, are born in a tightly confined area. Have you ever wondered why your dog loves to worm his way under a chair, table, or other tight space? Dogs look for spaces in your home or yard that mimic a den. Dog crates make excellent dens and provide that safe, secure environment dogs crave.

Using a crate is appropriate confinement—it's not punishment. Too many freedoms, too soon, is a recipe for failure. If your dog is young or immature, resistant to the rules, destructive in the home, or sometimes commits acts of aggression in the house, then judicious use of the crate is part of the solution. Until you have the time to devote to your dog's state of mind, your dog should be confined. In other words, if you are busy, distracted, or want to take a shower, your dog doesn't get free reign of the house. He has to be put into a safe, confined space like a crate, exercise pen, or kennel. No matter how good your pooch has been doing, unsupervised time in the house or yard is not in your pooch's best interest. Essentially, whenever your puppy or misbehaving dog is out of his crate or confined space, it's your time to *focus on* and *supervise* your dog and to provide an outlet for his mental and physical energy. That means you only have your dog out with you when you are able to pay attention and follow through. *All* other times of the day when you are not purposeful and intentional, your dog needs to be appropriately confined. Trust me, the time your dog is in his crate will provide you both with the ability to rest between purpose-driven activities.

It's not that this phase will last forever, but you have to prepare yourself that becoming balanced in your home is a process. Building the right relationship with your dog takes time. If you are meeting the required basics of purpose-driven activity with your pup or misbehaving dog, then the times that are appropriately confined are beneficial, fair, and reasonable.

*Crate Training Prep for Human*

Once my dog enters his crate, I do not get him out, regardless of the age of the dog. I don't pop back in to check on him or peer around the corner at him (he can smell you long before he sees you). This dog is safe, exercised, fed, watered, pottied, loved on…now he needs to rest and sleep. Dogs do not sleep without moving. They squirm, shuffle around, whimper, wake up, and sometimes even cry when they wake up—then they go back to sleep. If you react to every little noise, you are doing them a disservice and not allowing them to comfort themselves and go back to sleep. They would be ignored in their litter, and back to sleep they would go. If their mamas wouldn't acknowledge every noise made, we shouldn't either.

It's OK to hear the entire spectrum of noises when you put your pup or immature dog to bed: howling, yapping, crying, whining, whimpering, fever-pitch rantings, you get the idea. Typically, the noise can go on for ten to twenty minutes. Don't get a dog out until their appointed time in the schedule (more on this later). *Period.* The rare exception to this would be if my dog had been asleep and quiet for hours before suddenly beginning to *scream* as though a bear is eating him alive. That would get my attention, and I would go assess the situation and verify if a bear is in fact eating him. If a bear is not in the crate, simply turn and calmly walk away…and reposition your earplugs. If, however, you simply *have* to get them out because they are throwing a hissy fit that made you believe it was a bear in there, here's how it should be done.

1. Open the door like usual and do not allow him to bum-rush the door. I would wait for a polite pause and invite him out. NO affectionate touch, tone, or eye contact during this time, especially if he is agitated. It's routine as normal.
2. Put the leash on him immediately and go directly out to the designated potty spot.
3. Then quietly assess the dog to see if a bear did in fact peel the skin off his body.
4. Again, quietly lead him back into the house and return him directly into his crate, as usual. Take the leash off, close the door, and don't look back as you leave.
5. Yes, since they woke up, they could cry again for a while. Don't get them out! Don't acknowledge that fever-pitch state of mind!

I know how hard it can be to see this through, but it is so worth it in the end. My Kozi was the hardest dog to crate train in the world—or so I thought until I met a few others that almost convinced me that bears do eat dogs alive in their crates. Most dogs are content in their crates in less than a week with mere ten to twenty-minute crying jags. Kozi howled and screamed for *two weeks* straight and would cry for almost every moment in his crate. I thought I would die! I had to have my family sleep in our motorhome for two weeks. One weekend they even went to a motel! Kozi was tough to crate train. However, Kozi is my superstar now—he is a very bright, sensitive, and intense little guy! I'm certain that had I not stuck it out, Kozi could have become a neurotic dog with high anxiety. P.S. He *does* love his crate now! Quiet and calm, happy and peaceful!

Crate Training Benefits:

- People seriously underestimate a dog's need for rest, which is his time to think and use his brain. Being a good dog is very hard work! Rest is a critical element in training. Crate time allows a dog to soak up his lessons and recharge and reboot his mindset.
- Crate training has been proven to be the fastest and most effective way to housebreak a dog at any age. A dog's natural instinct is to avoid being near his own waste, so he'll make an effort to avoid eliminating in his crate. They learn this from their mamas!
- Crate training provides a safe, comfortable, and familiar place wherever you go (hotels, vet, groomer, etc.).
- Destructive behaviors are often the result of an unsupervised dog being bored or anxious. Using a crate during an owner's short-term absence eliminates this possibility. Dogs sleep the vast majority of the time when their owners are away anyway. Crating your dog while

you're away or unable to supervise keeps him from being destructive, stops nuisance behaviors, and prevents him from ingesting something that could potentially harm him.

Crate Training Dos:

- Make sure your crate is not too BIG! When potty training, it is imperative that the crate area your dog resides in is *very small*! It should only be big enough for a dog to stand up, turn around, and lie down.
- Introduce a crate to an older dog by feeding in it. You don't even have to leave the door closed for this. Just get the dog used to eating in there, and he'll soon look forward to when you unlatch the door. Move the food bowl deeper and deeper into the crate every day until your dog is happily eating inside. Then one day you can close the door until he's finished. You can delay opening the door by ten-minute intervals after that.
- Lock a dog out of the crate when it's not in use. Remove your dog, lock the door, and let him watch you toss a few yummy treats in there. Then walk away. He'll be counting the minutes until he can get in there! Then pop him in the crate while you do a quick errand or take a shower. Remember, the crate is not negotiable, but you are willing to make it fun.
- Adjust the location of the crate depending upon your dog. Some dogs do well in social areas like the living room; other dogs do better in a bedroom or basement where they are not distracted.
- Utilize the crate any time you are gone.
- Put a great chew toy in the crate like a Kong or a Busy Buddy or a pig's hoof. Use nothing digestible; we want the chewie to relieve stress, not contribute to the need for a dog to have an accident.

- Never make a big deal about letting your dog in or out of his crate. Wait until he's calm before releasing him from his crate and avoid giving praise or affection until he's relaxed.

Crate Training Don'ts:

- Never consider or use it as a form of punishment; rather consider it more like a safe place or puppy sitter—as long as it's a reasonable amount of time.
- Don't leave bedding in the crate if your dog is a destructive chewer. They can get an obstruction if swallowing bedding.
- Don't leave your dog in his crate for extended periods of time beyond what their age supports. For a dog under a year old, the general rule of thumb is age in months plus one hour. For example, a three-month-old puppy shouldn't be in a crate longer than four hours during the daytime. The nighttime stretch is generally an additional two to three hours to that general rule until they are making it through the night completely.

*Daily Schedule*

This schedule is created for puppies *and* dogs of all ages to be able to transition into your life in a successful way, but I have some special tips and tricks specific for puppies that I'll point out in my *Puppy Pit Stop* sections. Regardless of the age of your dog, regardless of the issues you are dealing with, this is the schedule we use at APBC to help shape, form, reboot, and reset a dog's perception of his world.

People always ask me how long this schedule needs to be followed. The answer: It's a maturity issue, not an age issue. When your dog is making mature choices on a consistent basis, even with little oversight from you, that's when you know you can let out some of the "choices rope." Just don't give so much they hang themselves, right! My older brother is ten years older than I am, and I sure do love him, but he still isn't mature. So there you go! Maturity is based on decisions, not age.

Structure, routine, boundaries, and earned affection are the keys to helping dogs of all ages and levels of training find comfort, grow in confidence, and find their place in our human world. Our schedule ensures consistency and purposefulness with your dog. It also ensures that when you are with your dog, you are providing an outlet for his mental and physical energy in a purposeful way. And finally, when things start to go awry with your dog down the road, this is the *exact* schedule you go back to for fourteen days. You'll be amazed at how quickly you see a huge difference. My Kozi—my trick master, my superstar, my blue-ribbon winning, cute-as-a-bugs-ear labradoodle—was out off leash a few months ago with my assistant trainer, and I called for Kozi to "come." My handsome boy popped his cute head out of a bush, looked right at me, promptly turned the other direction, and toodled off. I couldn't believe it, and my assistant looked at me, shaking her finger, and said, "Oh, he's so back in the program. Trust the process. It works." For goodness' sake, my assistant was quoting me to me! Lesson learned. Kozi boy was back in for his fourteen-day daily structure tune up.

Remember, it's not forever, but the longer you keep this structure and follow the guidelines set out in the Pillars of Pack Leadership program, the quicker your dog's behavior and your relationship with your dog will be everything you want it to be.

## *Daily Structure Sample*

Your dog's day is comprised of the following activities and suggested times. Be sure to fill in your times for your life. As your dog matures, you can extend Activity Times, and eliminate one of the crate times in the day's structure. I recommend that dogs of all ages have at least 2 crate times a day. If you work all day, you will need to hire a pet walker/care taker to help out in the middle of the day.

- *7am Wake up/potty time*: Potty rituals are for dogs of all ages, and their primary goal is to achieve immediate potty with no muss, no fuss. A potty ritual occurs *every time* your dog is taken out of his crate after a duration of 2 hours or more. You immediately go to the designated potty spot. Your pooch is on leash for all potty times. **Nothing else happens until potty happens.**
- *7:30am Feed Breakfast in crate.* Your dog is expected to sit and offer a polite pause before invited to eat.
- *8-11am Morning Activities*: Our mornings are comprised of short leash work, play, tethering during chores, e-collar work, pack walking, learning to JUST BE, and place.
- *11-1:30pm Crate time*: Feed Lunch in crate for puppies or dogs that need to gain weight
- *1:30pm Wake Up/Potty Time*
- *2-4:30pm Afternoon Activities*: Our afternoons are comprised of short leash work, play, tethering during chores, e-collar work, pack walking, place, learning to JUST BE, and beneficial socialization.
- *4:30-6:30pm Feed Dinner in Crate* Dcrate.
- *6:30pm Wake Up/Potty Time*
- *7-7:30pm* A nice walk or romp of play is perfect at this time of day.

- 7-9pm **End of Night Activities,** Your dog is in the house, on leash, resting and hanging out with you as you watch TV, read, or relax. This is a great time to groom, snuggle, tether, and work place.
- *9pm Potty Time*
- *Bedtime:* Into crate for the night

To summarize, Daily Structure is essential for your dog's mental and physical well-being. Naturally, as your dog matures, you can phase out some items and alter bedtimes, etc. Just know, that this is the schedule you come back to for 14 days whenever you need an attitude re-boot with your pooch. You'll know it's time to bring the Schedule for Success back if you find yourself saying something like, "I love my Fiona, she is amazing, smart, kind, lovely, and so good, almost all the time, EXCEPT FOR...."

!

***PUPPY PIT STOP:*** For eight-week-old puppies, bedtime is 8:00 p.m. I add a "late night potty" and "middle of the night" potty ritual that stretches out the potty time by thirty-minute progressions throughout the week. Day 1: 11 p.m. potty time, 4 a.m. potty time; Day 2: 10:45 p.m. potty time, 4:30 a.m. potty time; Day 3: 10:30 p.m. potty time, 5 a.m. potty time, and so on until the normal bedtime–7 a.m. routine is achieved successfully. At any point an accident in the crate occurs, you hold that time and do not stretch the interval until no accidents occur. Once there has been no accident, you can resume the thirty-minute stretch intervals until your pup can successfully hold it from bedtime potty time until your morning wake up. And yes, I do expect you to grow your pup's ability to move into your life's routine. I've had people alter their lives, beginning their day at 4 a.m. simply because their pup woke up at that time. A puppy may wake up during the night, but that does *not* mean you need to take that pup out to potty every time he makes a peep. Set the schedule, grow his ability to hold, and stick with it!

## *Rules to Live By*

To create a calm dog, we must start by creating a calm mindset before we move forward with any activity. It's never too early or too late to enforce or re-enforce these rules. Rules are never intended to completely exist on day one and completely cease to exist on day 15. You need to gradually begin fading the rules. NEVER completely stop them. And, when needed, you bring them ALL back into the forefront for a period of re-boot time. These rules help to create the safe, sane and civilized dog of your dreams. I have been profoundly affected by the work of training greats: Marc Goldberg, Chad Mackin and Heather Beck. These are things I've read and heard from them as I've trained with them through the years. Enjoy the wisdom of the decades.

1. Do not allow dogs on couches, sofas, and beds.
2. No toys readily available. If it's time to play, pull out a toy and interact with your dog. When play is over, put the toy away.
3. No begging and no table scraps.
4. No treats. Treats may come back, but for the beginning of training, we want the dog focused on you. Treats can easily overexcite and get the dog focused only on the food.
5. Do not give your dog attention when whining and barking and staring at you while doing it.
6. You initiate all the activities, helping your dog to learn that you control everything.
7. Walk ahead of your dog. Sit and sleep higher than your dog because position matters in a dog's mind.
8. You enter and exit first, dog second. Take time to calm your dog before you invite your dog to move in and out of doorways.
9. Your dog will remain in his crate unless being walked, tethered, played with, on place, or otherwise purposefully interacted with. This helps your dog understand that you control space. Most importantly, it gives you and your dog downtime to rest between purpose-driven activities.
10. Limit talking to your dog, as they do not understand words—they read our body language and the energy and focused intent behind it. Words can sometimes overexcite and create the opposite effect of what we want. Stay calm when working with your dog.

I'm often asked, "When can I stop following rule number…?" or "What will happen if I modify rule number…?" and I always tell this story. My Grandma Ruth had some treasured china cups that had been handed down through the generations. These precious cups were treasured in our family. On special occasions she would allow me the honor of having a tea party with them, but she wouldn't let me take these fragile treasures to my flimsy kiddie play table. I was only allowed to use them on her big, round oak table with these wonderful, thick, pillared legs. But imagine how stable that solid table would be if we started kicking out the legs. You get the picture. These rules to live by are critical to the continued balance and stability of your dog. They should not be kicked out on a one-by-one basis.

So keep in mind, these rules don't have to be forever, but they are what you come to when needed. The more of these rules you follow, the quicker your relationship with your dog will be everything you want it to be. Aly's recommended rules and structure helps to make—bad dogs good, good dogs great, and great dogs exceptional!

# Establishing Effective Rituals

In this section we will talk a lot about potty, feeding, and bedtime rituals. Rituals are defined as "solemn ceremonies or actions performed in a customary way." The reason these are so critical to your dog's life and state of mind is that they represent the major naturally occurring activities in a dog's daily life. He who controls the ritual, controls the status of the relationship. Consistently ritualizing your main events, such as potty, feed, and sleep habits, helps to keep your dog's stress down. You will have a calm, accepting, and respectful companion if you successfully implement these rituals. Your dog will be balanced and fulfilled in mind, body, and soul.

*Feed-Time Rituals*

Feed time is a ritual that allows you to give your dog another opportunity to "earn his keep," so to speak. In the animal kingdom, animals have to work for their food. It's up to us to create that same dynamic. Make sure your dog sits, politely pauses, and gives you a calm, accepting energy before you allow him to eat. He's earned it. Remember, in a dog pack the leader tells the dogs when to start and when to stop, and respect of space is *always* part of the equation. We have to create that same environment!

I feed dogs in their crates. Crates are an absolute *must* for families with more than one dog or with children around. You eliminate any chance of food aggression and food guarding issues when you feed in crate. I use this method right at first with pups and particularly with overly excited or food-dominant dogs. Crates are your best friend when it comes to helping an excited dog learn how to exhibit impulse control. Feeding in crates also reinforces how awesome crates are for the dog. It's their own comfy room with a stocked mini-bar…how much better does it get than that!

Remember, feed-time rituals are a time for you to establish order and appropriate balance in your relationship. Feed-time rituals begin and end with your influence. You say when it starts, and bowls come up when they are done. You ask for manners and only feed calm dogs. Do not panic if every morsel of food is not consumed at each meal. A healthy dog will *not* starve itself. Eventually, a dog adjusts to a work/eat/rest orderly schedule.

Feeding Ritual Benefits vs. Free feeding:

- You can easily monitor and regulate your dog's weight.
- You will know right away if your dog is not feeling well, because you will notice if his eating intake suddenly changes.
- Feeding rituals help with potty training.
- Feeding rituals help maintain a dog's food drive. Some dogs lose their food drive when food is available to them all the time.

Feeding Ritual Dos:

- Feed two times per day.
- Let your dog work for food by having him be polite and 'earn' his food.
- Feed your dog after some purpose-driven exercise—work, eat, rest.
- Create a routine and stick with it—dogs love this!

**PUPPY PIT STOP:** Puppies have different caloric and nutritional needs than older dogs, so you will feed them differently. Portion out your pup's daily total intake and divide into three or four small feedings a day, which should be adequate to meet the nutritional demands of your growing puppy. Make sure to up your food volume during growth spurts. Again, don't panic if every morsel isn't gone. A healthy puppy won't starve itself! For more information on food recommendations for your dog, see my section The Whole Dog.

*Bedtime Rituals*

The bedroom is a place for your dog…in the future. That kind of privilege needs to come when she has the maturity and impulse control to handle it. If you allow it too soon, she won't handle it well when that privilege is removed for whatever reason. For now, bed is in her crate, in a quiet space in your home. You need to rest and not be disturbed at every sound. And she needs to be able to cry and not be exposed to your reaction to it. She needs the safety and security of her crate. She needs to rest. She is not mature enough to handle free-roaming of the home. Eventually, your room, when invited, will be a wonderful place of relaxing and lounging. I have found that if you crate for the first year, a dog is emotionally prepared to handle the privilege of sleeping with her person and keeping the relationship in balance. Too much too soon will make the little pooch feel too powerful in your pack relationship. You will have to determine what your dog can handle. However, crates, like dens in the natural world, are the most calming and safe place your friend can have during her rest times. I drape a towel or blanket over a crate to create a den feeling. As I stated before, once my dog enters her crate for the evening, I do not get her out. For more information on crating, see my section *Crate Training Prep for Human*.

## Potty Rituals

Remember, rituals are predictable activities that lessen stress and anxiety in your dog because he knows he can count on you. Even going potty is a ritual that does far more for your dog than merely potty training him. Potty mistakes are a result of too much freedom and lack of appropriate confinement. Furthermore, punishing a potty accident actually increases their incidences. Accidents are not due to a dog's desire to go in the wrong spot. They are 100% due to a human's lack of supervision and not picking up or "reading" your dog's particular pre-potty clues.

<u>Potty Rituals Dos:</u>

- Take your dog to the potty spot after being in his crate for a sustained period of time (2–4 hours).
- Put his leash on and go directly to the potty spot.
- When an accident occurs (not if, but when), *completely clean up the soiled area!* Use white vinegar! You don't want to leave any scent residue, or it will become a new potty spot.
- Praise your dog calmly and gently *after* going potty.

<u>Potty Ritual Don'ts:</u>

- Don't do anything to distract your dog from getting to business. It's not play time. It's not talk time. It's not pet-your-dog time. It's get to business, quietly and efficiently.
- After an accident occurs, *do not punish!* If you try to punish or correct a dog after the fact, it's simply too late. You must catch a dog in the act, or else your dog cannot perceive the connection between the mess and your frustration.

- Don't rub a dog's nose in the mess; it's unsanitary and disgusting.

- Don't think that a dog "knows" he did something wrong because he looks guilty. He's learned to associate a mess with your frustrated response.

- Don't ever take a dog's behavior personally. Just re-evaluate what went wrong and what you could do differently to make the better behavior easier for your dog to execute.

For healthy dogs, that's it, gang. Also…

***PUPPY PIT STOP:*** Crate times throughout your day, as outlined in your schedule, is the secret to effective potty training and to helping our little one learn how to hold. The biggest mistake I see people make is taking pups out too often and ruining any chance at growing a pup's ability to hold his business. I've heard this time and time again from my clients: After an accident happens, they start running a pup out to potty every hour instead of sticking to the schedule. Eventually, you'll begin to read your dog very well. And if you are doing tethering (more on this later) as prescribed, you'll be ready to notice when your pup looks like he is about to go. If a pup has an accident while tethered to you, then that is on *you*, not the pup! If you are supervising your pup (and he doesn't have free-roaming rights too soon), you really will learn the rhythms of your pup and his potty needs. When a pup opens his eyes from sleeping and comes out of any appropriately confined space after being there for a sustained block of time (2–4 hours), then put a leash on him and go directly out to the designated potty place. Finally, when potty training a pup, controlling access to water is essential. Do not leave water in the crate. Do not have free access to water after 7:00 p.m.

# Mastering Purpose-Driven Activities

### *Walking*

How we exercise our dogs matters. My friend, Cheri Lucas, a well-known dog behaviorist, clinician, and founder of Second Chance for Love rescue organization, often states, "Birds fly, fish swim, and dogs walk." Walking is what dogs *do*. Dogs need to walk, and we need to walk them—that is our part of the deal! A dog walking or running around a backyard alone is not a purpose-driven activity. When left alone in a yard, a dog will usually nap a lot, and don't be surprised if your dog discovers nuisance and destructive behaviors when left alone. Even if your yard is large and safe, having your dog out there isn't giving your dog the social connection he needs and for his desires to be fulfilled. A purpose-driven walk provides everything that fulfills your dog's mind, heart, and soul. It's the way dogs work in a pack. When done right, the purpose-driven walk will:

- Earn you a position of leadership with each step you take
- Drain your dog's excess energy
- Help you practice a social ritual of migration with your dog
- Fulfill your dog's emotional need for connection
- Serve as a form of affection for your dog

I recommend at least two brisk, structured walks averaging anywhere between fifteen minutes to an hour every day, depending upon your dog's age and fitness level. Just imagine, you are helping your own health as you establish and deepen a healthy relationship with your dog! I call it a great two-for-one deal!

***PUPPY PIT STOP:*** With our puppies, the conversation shouldn't be, "Don't take your pup anywhere until they are older than sixteen weeks." The conversation should be, "Take your pup to as many low-risk places as possible." Yes, you can—and should—take a puppy on a purpose-driven walk; it's just a matter of knowing the difference between low-risk and high-risk areas. Low-risk places have a low volume of unknown or unhealthy dogs and have less exposure to grass and dirt, which is where bad viruses live best and prosper. Examples of low-risk places: Aunt Sue's house with her older, inoculated dog, Fifi, and your neighborhood sidewalks. Conversely, high-risk places to avoid are environments that have a high influx of unknown dogs and dirt and grass present. Examples of high-risk places: A dog park, dog beach, big-box pet store, and popular dog trails.

One of the reasons people are told not to take their puppies under sixteen weeks of age out on walks is because they are vulnerable to scary diseases like parvo and distemper. However, the risk of *not* appropriately socializing and exposing your young pup to sights, sounds, smells, and textures in that critical developmental time of eight to sixteen weeks old carries far greater risks than your pup actually contracting those dreaded diseases. There is a far greater number of dogs that are euthanized because they were under-socialized or inappropriately socialized vs. dogs that die from parvo and distemper. For more information, please check out the American Veterinary Society of Animal Behavior's statement detailing how essential socialization is (a link is available on our website at www.alysonrodges.com).

## BEFORE YOU WALK:

Before you begin your walk, grab a 3–4-foot leash and a properly fitted collar—and no, not the collar your tags are on! There are a myriad of collars and tools, and you can contact your local professional to help you find the one that is most effective for you and to have it fit correctly. Tools are neutral. It's the hands that use them that define whether they are positive or negative, effective or ineffective. As you head out, your dog will want to follow you around, so encourage it, but just be sure that you have her walking *behind you or near your side*, entering doors upon invitation, and respecting your space wherever you are present. Respecting your space means not barging ahead of you into a door or ramming into you when she wants to get your attention (more on this later). Don't forget, dogs like order and are naturally wired to respond to it. Good leadership isn't about domination or robot-like control; it's about providing healthy balance, structure, discipline, and order. In the words of my mentor, the IACP Hall of Fame dog trainer and ForceFree™ Method creator, Marc Goldberg, "You are forming a partnership—you just want to ensure that you are the senior partner!" With all this in mind, it's time to get moving—go on…get walking!

> **PUPPY PIT STOP:** When you are about to head out to your low-risk, safe place with your 8–16-week-old pup, take a leash that has a longer lead, from 6–10 ft., so your puppy can drag it along as you move whenever you need to drop the line. Your collar can be a flat collar for this dragline work (more on this later).

## HOW TO WALK:

*You*: Head up, shoulders up, arms down by your sides, with hands relaxed, holding leash softly in your hand. If you can touch your ear whenever you apply pressure to your leash, your hands are acting crazy! Don't tense up when you are moving in any direction.

A common mistake humans make is grabbing a leash tighter, preparing to turn or to stop, or approaching something that makes you uncomfortable (or you think might make your dog uncomfortable). *Relax!* Wiggle your fingers and chicken-wing flap your arms and elbows periodically to remind yourself to loosen up. If you are a person who tends to have "crazy arms," you can do this little trick: Butterfly your leash up so that you are holding your leash at its correct length all in one hand (the side near your dog). Then, with hands still holding the leash, put your thumb inside your pocket! It's an old dog-trainer trick to keep you from using your hands inappropriately.

*Dog*: Your dog should walk alongside or slightly behind you on a loose leash. Dogs cannot be smelling, marking, fixating—all activities that reduce your authority while walking. Believe me, dogs can smell their world as they walk along without having their head stuck to the ground or wandering off! If your dog starts to be silly and inappropriate on your walk, you have techniques to improve his behavior! Shutting down the silliness (as described earlier), strategically using stops (and waiting for calm), left turns, right turns, and about-face turns can help refocus a dog's attention back to you. Walks are intended to be experienced together. It's no fun when you are walking and talking with your friend and she has her nose stuck to her cellphone. That feels rather disconnected, right? It's no different if your dog is completely tuned out from you and totally absorbed in his own world.

If your dog is pulling ahead relentlessly, throw in an about-face turn or sharp left turn. Try this:

- Begin briskly walking in a forward motion on a straight line about twenty feet.
- Relax your arms (don't get tight—remember the "thumb in the pocket" trick?) and execute a sharp 180-degree turn

(keeping on your straight line). Continue walking along on your straight line. Remember to breathe and relax as you are moving along. If your dog starts to forge ahead, again, repeat the sequence, randomizing your speed and how far you go before you execute the next turn.

- Suddenly execute a 90-degree turn to the left, walking forward fifteen steps, repeating the sequence until you've marched a sharp square, then take off on another line of walking. If your dog is lagging behind, take off at a jog for thirty steps and then throw in an about-face turn.
- Then throw a sharp 90-degree right turn in, making a nice small square comprised of right turns before you head out on another straight line.
- See our *Puppy Pit Stop* tips below if your dog is resistant to the leash—these tips also work wonderfully for dogs of all ages!

The goal of using your stops and turns is to strategically interrupt your dogs silliness *before* it escalates and to get your dog thinking and caring more about where the heck you are going. Mix it up, practice, use your stops, left turns, right turns, and about-face turns strategically, interrupting the flow of your dog's direction to help him tune back into you. Don't *drill* and *kill* your dog with your turns and stops. Use them wisely. Use them intermittently and strategically. Reward and praise your dog when he does tune into you, continually encouraging the "check in." And keep practicing. Your dog will soon be motivated to tune into you, and your walk will be a wonderful experience for you both.

In addition to the traditional short-leash walk, you can most certainly add dragline and long-line work for puppies eight weeks and older and for dogs of different ages and levels of training that are resistant to respecting leash pressure. A dragline is merely a long leash that needs to be a minimum of 6 feet, and you can go longer. I use lines from 6–25 ft. To do dragline work, drop the line and let the pup or dog drag it along as you move. For long-line work, hold the end of the line as you move. Lines need to be made out of a lighter material like nylon so that it's not too heavy. Lines made out of chain can startle your pup, and leather lines may entice a puppy to chew it! Both kinds of line work help a dog learn to move along with you in a no-pressure, fun way. Long lines help dogs learn to move out away from you and grow confidence as they experience new smells, sights, and sounds, yet stay tuned into you as you move along. Draglines are perfect for puppies that might resist any pressure on the line, as they have more of a sense of freedom, yet you still have enough line to ensure that you can step on it, scoop it up, or grab it in an emergency, influencing your dog's choices from a distance.

Dragline Dos

- Always observe your pup or dog when a dragline is on. Your pooch could easily get hooked on something and choke.
- Use the dragline in the house to prevent your puppy or dog from sneaking off into an unobserved area to get into mischief or have a potty accident.
- Scoop up the dragline occasionally when your pooch is enthusiastically moving along with you, and immediately drop it if the pup or dog resists. Your pooch will like it when you encourage her to move along with you without force.
- Step on the dragline, offer a treat, and encourage your pup or dog to come. If she seems to not want to come to you, gently reel her in to clarify what you wanted her to do.

### Dragline Don'ts

- Never attach a dragline to anything other than a flat collar. No restricting collars.
- Never allow children to tease your pup or dog or to drag them along on the dragline.
- Never allow your pup or dog to chew the dragline. You can squirt her with a water bottle if she thinks it's a fun new game.

\* \* \*

## AFTER YOU WALK:

At the end of a wonderful, polite, respectful walk, it is certainly appropriate to reward your dog with some "free smell" time! It's your way of letting Fluffy know that you appreciate her good behavior as she walked nicely along with you. Find a nice spot, relax, and allow her to smell the roses (or the fire hydrant) for a few minutes. Just make sure that your "relax" time isn't greater than the time you actually were focused on your purpose-driven walk!

At the end of the day, your relationship with your dog is up to you. Walking is one of the most important things you can do with your dog to help the relationship be healthy, balanced, and reciprocated.

### *Tethering*

Tethering is a very important part of any training program! It helps a dog tune in to you and learn how to JUST BE right along with you as you live your life. Put a leash on a dog, hold onto the leash with your hand or hook to your belt, and simply go about your business. Insist that your dog *not pull* you around the house and rather accompanies you as you move around. Tethering is about calm, quiet togetherness, not about play, excitement, or affection. If you sit down to do some bookwork, your dog should be near you. Tethering is a quiet exercise—*no commands are given.* He decides if he sits, stands, or lies down. Tethering is not an affection exercise, so do not talk to or touch your dog during this process. If he nudges or jumps on you, use your leash to move him slightly away from you. Before long, he'll learn how to appreciate just being with you without being fussy or demanding.

Tips for Tethering:

- If the door sends your dog into a state of crazy, make frequent tethered walks to the door, get a sit, and wait for calm. Then leave the door area.
- Practice tethering when your dog has already had some exercise and isn't pent up with energy.
- If your dog jumps or is pesty, just keep using your leash to move him away from you. You can also use a Pet Convincer to give him a blast of forced air if he is a repeat jumping offender.
- Tether your dog to you three to five times a day for twenty minutes or more! Tether when you are working in the garden, sweeping, mopping, dusting, doing laundry, cleaning dishes, working on the computer, making phone calls, watching TV, reading a book, etc.
- Let your dog decide his own position as you are tethering. If you stop and read a book, he decides if he lies down, sits, or stands. The goal is that your dog will eventually choose to immediately default to a relaxed and calm position of his own choosing when you are busy or otherwise involved in an activity.

## Using a Treadmill

A treadmill is a great way to get your dog a dose of healthy indoor exercise—if conditioned to it appropriately! First, allow your dog to get comfortable with the sight and sound of a running treadmill. Next, place your dog on the treadmill and give him a treat. Once your dog is adjusted, you can gradually increase the speed to provide a more challenging workout.

Treadmill Dos:

- Make sure your dog is *consistently* responding to soft leash pressure, meaning if there is the slightest forward pressure on the leash, your dog responds appropriately by moving forward. You want to be certain that if your dog meets pressure on the leash, he doesn't stop and throw his weight backwards.
- Use the "paws up" command and entice your dog to walk onto the treadmill of his own volition.
- Once on treadmill, be prepared with your leash hand in the front of the treadmill to help guide the first steps and have a treat handy to help entice forward motion.
- Turn treadmill on and gently encourage your dog with forward motion. No jerking motion with your hands, just mere guidance to keep him centered on treadmill. If he does want to stop walking, your hand (and treat and verbal encouragement) is there reinforcing the lead to encourage him forward.
- Start at a slow speed and move the speed up so your dog is walking at a regular stride. In time you can increase the speed so your dog is comfortably jogging.
- Look for your dog's calm state of mind *before* you invite him off of a treadmill. Do not think you can run the crazy out of a dog on a treadmill. Won't happen. If your dog is acting crazy, you'll just get the most fit, crazy dog in the world

- that can maintain his level of crazy for unending amounts of time without ever panting!
- The goal is to affect the mindset of your dog with purposeful treadmill work.

Treadmill Don'ts

- DO NOT LEAVE YOUR DOG ALONE ON A TREADMILL—*EVER!*
- Do not tie your dog to a treadmill.
- Do not go too long. I put ten-week-old pups on a treadmill for sixty seconds. I put dogs over a year on a treadmill for approximately fifteen minutes.

*Playing*

All good games have rules, and playing with your dog is no different. There is no limit to the types of games you can play with your dog. If he likes it and you like it, turn it into a game. Just ensure that the game begins and ends upon your invitation and that there are rules to your play. For example, if you want to play fetch, great! Make sure your dog comes back to you and sits. You can throw a toy and have a dog bring it back to place, and trade a treat for the toy, working on "get it, bring it, leave it." Remember, no game is fun if a bully shows up or if the rules are broken. *Never allow rude or inappropriate behavior while playing your game.*

How do you know if play is appropriate? If you can interrupt a play session by stepping into a dog's space while applying indirect pressure *and your dog acknowledges you*, that is a good indicator he is in the correct mindset with the correct energy. Play time isn't "lose your brain" time for your dog. Games should be able to pause and then resume. Be wise and bring play into check *before* things spin out too much. Even when dogs are playing with other dogs, step in *before* things go too far. If he gives you a blow-off acknowledgement (kind of like a "yeah, yeah, yeah, don't bother me" attitude), try stepping into your dog's space and keeping the indirect pressure up until he yields, offers a sit, or he lies down. Then, allow play to resume.

Your "check in" is essential in helping dogs maintain a balanced state of mind. The most important part of checking in is that you must be willing and prepared to enforce rules—always. If your dog ignores or runs away from you, purposeful play has mutated into something *not beneficial* to your relationship. Get a leash or long line back on your dog during play so that you can apply direct pressure to get the respectful pause in the game. Once you've achieved it, great! Back to your game you go!

*Using Place*

"Place, place, place." What the heck is it, and why should you use it with your pooch? I use place daily in my training with *every* puppy and dog. I use it because it teaches a dog and a human how to be better connected and how to have a calm state of mind. A tall order for sure, but truly, place done right does achieve those goals.

Place is a defined space with a clear boundary. A dog is expected to remain on a specific place until invited off. It can be a dog bed, a blanket, mat, folded towel, sweatshirt, or anything comfortable. I use raised dog beds when training place for two reasons: 1) Dogs love them. They are comfortable, warm in winter, and cool in summer. 2) Most importantly, these raised beds make it abundantly clear to both the dog and the human when the dog is getting off.

The use of place helps to lay the foundation in your dog for so many things: patience, impulse control, a future down or sit with duration, the ability to be calm in the face of a known trigger (like doorbells or food), relaxation, overall calm state of mind, respect of space, just to name a few. Place is where a dog can relax, chill out, get softly brushed, etc. Place is the place where all good things happen!

Here is what place is not: Place is not a spot to play with toys when working the command. Place is not punishment. Place is never used in anger or commanded with an angry or cautionary tone. Place is not a grueling order like a military "stand at attention" until you break emotionally or physically. Supervision is still very much a part of place—it's not a spot for you to leave and forget about your dog. Place is not optional; it begins and ends upon your invitation.

You begin using place with a dog in very small doses. I put a pup or dog on place at the beginning of a commercial and invite him off at the end of the commercial. Then I go for two commercials and build from there. Eventually, you can easily have a pup or dog successfully on place for an hour or so, as you watch a movie, sweep the patio, or pull weeds.

You guide your dog by giving direction from your leash or dog's collar as you walk purposefully toward the designated place until all four paws are on, simultaneously saying the command "place." Every once in a while, toss a treat onto place so your dog will magically find a treat there. It's the dog's choice to stand, sit, or lie down. He just can't get off. Once on place, be sure to release all leash or collar pressure. The goal to work toward is being able to keep your dog on place without holding onto the leash and until he is invited off. Yes, that does mean that if even one paw comes off, you need to put him back on place *immediately*. And yes, that means *every time* he gets off uninvited.

I ask humans to use as few words as possible while pooch is on place. I am asking both dog and human to begin to clue in to each other and to be aware of what is going on. If pooch looks like he is going to step off, relax and breathe as you move in toward him, giving him a warning sound. If he stays on and looks at you, relax and take half a step back. If you need to, use leash pressure to put him back on place. Then, as he is able to tolerate it, keep stepping half a step back slowly. Keep breathing!

Once place is firmly established in your dog's life and helps to promote a calm mindset in your dog, you can begin to add novel movements, sounds, and distractions. Gradually, you will add things that "trigger" your dog, such as: doorbells, open doors, food, other dogs, toys, bicycles riding by, etc. while they remain on place. It's not enough to tell your dog, "No, don't chase after that toy or bolt out the door." You have to show him the right thing to do instead when faced with that exciting stimuli. Place is the place where dogs can comfortably tap into calm, even in the face of things that used to send them to the stratosphere.

How you exit place is as important as the calm you have achieved while on it. When you have your dog calm, quiet, and relaxed, that is when you go to him, gently massage him, and quietly take his leash and step off a few steps, finishing in a quiet sit. By not talking or barking out commands, you are actually helping your dog maintain all the calm that was achieved while on place. When you begin to move off place, should your dog decide to stay, just keep moving with steady pressure until pooch comes along with you. One of the reasons you have your dog's leash on is so you can offer a bit more guidance if needed. Ultimately, *not coming* when invited is not on the list of available options!

Place teaches our dogs as much as it teaches us. Both partners are learning patience, consistency, and mutual understanding, as well as how to read each other's body language better. It's a powerful thing when we establish a calm state of mind and clear lines of communication with our dog, and when we learn how to do it with no words at all—*priceless!*

# Establishing Respect of Space and Creating Space Boundaries

Dogs don't speak English, Spanish, or French. They speak spatially. However, dogs are keenly intuitive and desire to know the intentions of other dogs and humans. They interact with each other by moving into or away from another dog's space (pressure on/pressure off). *How* they enter that space is their correct or incorrect understanding of social dynamics, respect of space issues, and their ability to interpret intent accurately.

Respect is everything in a dog's world. A dog may love you, but may not respect you. Conversely, a dog may fear you, but may not respect you. Earning a dog's respect is critical for developing and maintaining a balanced relationship. Respect is a precursor for trust, a calm state of mind, and for the ability to make good choices.

Respect of space and acknowledgement of the pack leader are essential first growth steps for you and your dog. It is up to you, the pack leader, to establish that relationship immediately upon welcoming a new member to your pack. A dog processes his world through his nose, eyes, ears, and most especially through recognizing the energy that a pack member is directing toward him.

I use very few words when I begin working with a dog. I'm not concerned with obedience to a command at this point. In a calm, firm manner, I have a very directed intent on a dog. Believe me, a dog will sniff out insincerity or lack of conviction in a millisecond. The only state of mind I am interested in is a calm, compliant, and accepting one. It's the only state of mind that gets any attention from me at all. Good things come to those dogs that choose *calm!* I always envision that I have a Hula-Hoop around me (the size of the hoop is up to your imagination), and a dog may not enter my Hula-Hoop until invited. I picture my Hula-Hoop at every door, every chair, every stair, every entranceway, every elevator—you get the idea—and that dog may not proceed until I give him the go-ahead. If he infringes upon my Hula-Hoop space, I move into him, applying indirect pressure until he yields and stops the forward progression. And then, when the dog does move, he must move in a controlled fashion, not an overly excited leap into me. Dogs and pups can approach respectfully!

Doors are a perfect opportunity to enforce and reinforce respect of space and to create space boundaries! How many times do you go in and out of a threshold in one day? Yep, you guessed it—tons! (Creating threshold respect is a safety issue as well, as a door-bolting dog could become a dead dog.) You have *many* opportunities to establish a calm mindset in your dog just by moving around your house. Ask your dog to sit, *wait* for a polite pause, and create that respect of space at the door. You establish the state of mind your dog will be in on the other side of the door before you even walk through it!

# MASTERING THE HUMAN PART OF THE EQUATION

This one is all about you—the human component! The minute you welcome a dog into your life, a conduit of information flow has been established between you and your dog. Your emotions factor into the state of mind of your dog in a significant way. It's very important that you have the right perspective about how you will interact with your pooch. She should not be the center of your universe. It is a *ton* of pressure on a dog to be the end all, be all of a human's life. That kind of intense scrutiny and interaction is way too much for her, and she will be relieved that she doesn't have to play that role in your life. As you've worked your way through this guide, your dog is just now beginning to learn how to JUST BE. She is figuring out that the pleasures in life exist because she can JUST BE.

Dogs are *very* intuitive and responsive to us, and I know this is not easy to hear, but they often reflect what is going on inside of *us*. If we are overly concerned about anything (including too concerned for the dog itself), or if the dog is over-the-top in any area (like not letting an owner out of her sight), it is more of a reflection of what is going on in her owner's head than in hers. People will say, "Oh look, she's mad at me." "Oh, poor baby is scared." "Oh, she can't live without me; she goes crazy if she's out of my sight." "She knows she did something wrong." When you say things like that, it usually means that *your* emotions are being reflected back to you by your pooch.

You see, your dog is a dog. Period. And although they may not process the world the same way we do, they most certainly will react to all our visible and non-visible emotions. Sure, they have good days, bad days, preferences, favorite things, just like us, but we often use their negative emotions as excuses for allowing inappropriate choices and behavior from them. After all, we have to go to work and perform duties in a safe, sane, and civilized way, even when we don't really want to. It ought to be the same for your dog.

We humans must acknowledge that the needs of a dog are not the same as the needs of a human. Dogs love to live in the moment. Yes, a dog is a devoted companion, and when there is balance in the relationship, it's a healthy, wonderful, reciprocated devotion. However, I'll hear people say, "I just want a lap dog, someone to snuggle with." My response: get a stuffed animal to squeeze and touch all the time. Dogs don't do that in their world. Balanced dogs don't follow another dog around incessantly with eyes glued to the other dog, whining and crying. Balanced dogs relax, hang out around each other, lie down, rest; sometimes they'll romp for a bit, snuggle, then they will JUST BE. So if we truly want the best for our dogs, we need to lead by example and help them to become the calm, relaxed, balanced, happy dogs they were meant to be.

*Touch, Tone, Timing, and Energy*

You will hear me say over and over and over: "Touch, tone, timing, and energy." Mastering these elements will truly make you the best pack leader and senior partner in your relationship with your pooch. Every touch of your leash, every nuanced tone of your voice, every touch of your fingers, every look you give, every move of your body is saying something to your dog. Your job is to ensure that you are saying *exactly* what you mean to say. Your job is to ensure that you are enforcing or reinforcing *exactly* the state of mind you desire in your dog.

## TOUCH

We humans touch dogs a lot. Often in ways they really don't care for. But in our ignorance, bliss, or selfishness, we touch anyway. I can't tell you how often I've heard a client tell me, "I want to pet him to tell him I love him and that he did a good job." And usually, that dog would have preferred a smile and small scratch under the chin. Most dogs hate being hugged. Many dogs will tolerate it with grace—the smiling face of the family golden retriever with a child's arms wrapped around its neck comes to mind. But some dogs will feel threatened, fearful, or just flat-out loathe the feeling, and in fact, a child grabbing a dog for a hug is why many dog bites occur. Most dogs dislike being touched on top of the head or on the muzzle, ears, legs, paws, and tail. Additionally, our touch often sabotages the very state of mind we seek in our dogs. Imagine this: You've asked your dog for a down. Your dog plops into his down, and you immediately jump down there and enthusiastically pet him. He suddenly jumps up from his down, excitedly wagging his tail. Your touch, what you perceive as a heartfelt "Good boy! Job well done!" for going into his down, actually turned into the very thing that made him disobey and pop up from his down. That doesn't seem very fair.

For most dogs, a gentle scratch under the chin is usually appreciated. Slow petting, similar to gentle massage or light scratching, can calm a dog down. Place your hand on an area where the dog enjoys being handled and gently move your hand or fingers in the same direction the fur grows. I think the greatest praise we can ever give our dogs is to take the time to notice what kind of touch they actually enjoy. Let's set our dogs up for success by being mindful about when we touch our dog and by considering the kind of touch that is beneficial to their state of mind.

## TONE

A recent scientific study verified what dog trainers have always known—that what we say to our dogs matters, how we say it matters, and when we say it matters.

"A recent study conducted at [Sussex University] found that similarly to humans, the verbal and non-verbal (vocal) elements of speech are processed in different areas of the brain. The researchers were looking at the dog's response to hemispheric biases—left vs. right brain when processing their response to human speech….Subtle variations in your speech pattern or tone of voice, could illicit an opposite response, or reduced response to the task requested….Perhaps your non-verbal intonation pattern had a subtle change in: 1) Volume (loud-soft) 2) Rate (fast-slow) 3) Pitch (high-low) Upward-high; Downward-low Circumflex (high to low; low to high) Even a subtle difference may have communicated a confusing or different request, and therefore, a different response" (Thompson).

Now that science has confirmed what we dog people have observed for years—that the tone of our voice influences are dog's understanding and response—let me give you an example of how tone used incorrectly can sabotage your dog's good choices.

You are ready to go out for a walk and start to say in a high-pitched, excited voice, "You ready to go for a walk? Mama is ready! Let's get your leash. Come on, let's go!"—and with each increased pitch of your happy voice, your dog gets more and more excited and starts to spin around and jump. Then you wonder why your dog is pulling like a nut on your leash as you head out for your walk.

It's important that we admit when we weren't clear or didn't do something correctly and just fix the issue without wasting time being upset about it. We have to own our part of the equation in our dog's behavior. We need to say what we mean and say it in a way that sets our dogs up for success. A calm, even, authoritative tone makes your requests clear and understandable to your dog and avoids sending mixed signals.

## TIMING

Timing is always very critical in training any animal. Whether it be timing of a correction, timing of a treat, or timing of a release of indirect or direct pressure. Release is how the dog knows that he made the right choice and did the right thing. Through the years there have been several studies trying to determine the exact amount of time between the desired action and the timing of the reinforcement to get the desired result of understanding with your dog. The general consensus is—be quick with your praise and treats!

One of the ways we communicate with our dogs is how we respond to them. The timing of those responses can be critical to making sure we are sending the message we intend. Since our dogs don't understand language like we do, we don't have the option of simply explaining what we want from them. It becomes more like a game of charades, where we have to catch them doing something right (or something wrong) and help them understand that the behavior they are doing is something we want (or don't want). It's a tricky thing and made even more complicated if our timing isn't good. Being consistent and timely in our rewards/corrections will help reinforce the behavior we are looking for.

## ENERGY

Your energy is also essential. I'll even go so far as to call it authentic energy! You simply cannot lie to a dog. You can tell me that you are calm and relaxed until the cows come home, but if that dog knows you're nervous, we will see it in your dog. You can tell me that you want the dog to stay on place, but when it tests you thirty times by trying to get off, you've got an authenticity issue.

Remember when you were a kid and your mom called you to "get in the house!"—and you knew she meant it the last time. *How* did you know she meant it? She called you three times before that, but on that final time, you knew you were in for trouble if you didn't high-tail it home. It's this simple: You need to mean what you say, say what you mean—the first time. And remember, you don't have to be mean to mean it.

*Body Language: Putting It All Together*

The first thing to do on this journey of self discovery and development of effective touch, tone, timing, and energy is to watch your body language—and that of dog trainers you love—when working your dog. Have a friend or family member video you working your dog. Watch videos, tons of videos. Watch a dog trainer's every body move with a discerning eye. I post videos daily on my Facebook page, Aly's Puppy Boot Camp, so that my client's can watch our team working with dogs every day. It is up to you to learn about the importance of body language. No one can learn this for you. You simply have to get in there and start doing it to the best of your ability. To be effective with your dog, you have to wrap your brain around the fact that everything you do impacts your dog—your touch, tone, timing, and energy. Trust me when I tell you…this takes time. But it's so worth it! You are learning a foreign language called *dog*, and it takes an understanding of the art of movement and how it's applied.

Here are a few things to watch for when studying yourself and different trainers on video—happy homework!

- Watch the body language of the dogs as they are worked. Are they relaxed or tight?
- See the hand position and amount of pressure being applied on the leash. Is the handler's hand position level

with the dog's nose? Higher, above the head? Off to the side?

- Notice the angle of the human's body in relation to the dog's. Is it facing directly toward the dog or sideways? On the side or in front of the dog?
- What is the distance from the dog—close or distant?
- When does the handler look at the dog? When does the handler look away?
- When does the handler step forward (apply pressure)? When does the handler step back (release pressure)?
- Where do the handler's hands move—up, down, or to the side? How quickly—fast or slow? Smooth? Steady or jerking pressure?
- What was happening with the dog when the handler moved his or her hands?
- When did the handler touch the dog? What happens to the dog when touched? Does the dog lean away/look away from the handler when touched? Or does the dog move toward the handler when touched?
- When is a word spoken to the dog? What is being said? (Hint: Look for "name and explain" or "marking" techniques—every time I say *hi* or *good* or *yes*, that is a marker for something specific we've seen in a dog's decision.)
- When is a treat given? What happens to the dog when treated? Is the dog growing calmer, more focused, or does the dog get more excited?
- Good dog communicators *breathe*. Notice when they exhale.
- When does the handler move into a strong standing position with hands on hips?
- Where are the handler's feet? (Together or slightly apart and angled?)

- When does the handler make directional changes? When does the handler move forward, backward, sideways? When does the handler turn left, right, or about-face?
- When is the handler standing still? How long?

The overarching truth is that you are saying something to your dog at all times, you just have to be certain that your touch, tone, timing, and energy are all saying what you intend to say.

# COMMANDS

Commands come *after* the relationship is established. I always say to my clients that once you can get a dog—and especially puppies—to do all the behaviors you desire *with no words at all*, then you are ready to add your "commands." Remember, the Pillars of Pack Leadership helps you learn all the ways to build relationship, clarity, and understanding and to gain your dog's acceptance. *Only then* do you train commands. As I said earlier, dogs don't speak English, Spanish, or Japanese—at least not in the way you think they do! They speak a spatial language with nuanced reading of intent. They respond to all kinds of pressures, encouragement, and discouragement. Most domesticated dogs have a vested interest in discerning our intent and try to use all their innate knowledge to learn what the heck we want from them.

*Leash-Handling Basics*

Before we begin with commands, we need to understand a few leash-handling basics. First, use just your thumb. Slip your thumb through the loop at the end of the leash then fold the leash in your hand. Close your hand. Do not wrap the leash around your hand, wrist, or arm. For maximum control and safety, make sure the leash is coming out of the bottom of your hand (near your pinky finger) when you are finished folding. There should also be enough slack between your hand and your dog so your dog is not uncomfortable. Hold your arms down at your sides, not bent upwards or even above your head. If you stop to talk to someone or give the dog a break, either put a foot on the leash or hold it with your hands together as though you're holding a baseball bat and keep the leash braced against your belly button so the dog doesn't pull you around.

Before we start pulling on a leash willy-nilly, let's first learn about positions and the best way to apply leash pressure. One of my dog-training heroes, Chad Mackin, shared this method with me, and I've found it the easiest way to explain it to my clients: Picture your dog standing on your left side. Now picture that your dog's body has the positions of the face of a clock. Your dog's head is 12 o'clock, his tail is 6, his left side is 9, and his right side is 3.

Before you ever begin applying leash pressure, you need to have your hand at the correct distance from your dog's body in order to have appropriate leverage. Place your guiding hand (left hand if your dog is on your left) so it is 8–10 inches up the leash from your dog's collar. People often have their hands too far up the leash and lose leverage. When you are ready to apply direct pressure on the leash, you need to apply that pressure in the most effective direction.

For example, getting your dog to sit, apply gentle pressure straight up above the dog's head into the 12 o'clock position. The millisecond he sits, *immediately* release the pressure. The release of pressure is praise for the dog so he can understand that he made the right choice. Want to turn left? Apply gentle pressure in the 9 o'clock direction. Want to turn right? Apply gentle pressure in the 3 o'clock direction. Tie your leash to a doorknob and practice moving your hands up and down your leash so you can smoothly, quickly, and effectively get your hands to their proper position on the leash, about 8–10 inches from the doorknob. Yes, you do have to learn how to take up slack, let slack out, and use both your hands while doing it. You have to be able to quickly and efficiently get your hands up and down your leash in a smooth way. Practice!

Okay, now that you are able to smoothly move your hands into their correct positions, here is a list of the commands I utilize, their definitions, and some pointers on how to achieve each command.

In each skill set, gradually increase difficulty and fade and randomize treats.

SIT: Tells your dog to sit. Using just two fingers on the leash, apply gentle pressure in the 12 o'clock position and maintain steady pressure until the sit occurs. The millisecond your dog's butt hits the ground, immediately release the pressure. Another thing I like to do is to slowly move a treat from just in front of the dog's nose, then up and back over her muzzle (a couple of inches away from her head) to between her eyes. As soon as your dog's butt hits the ground, mark it with a "yes," praise her, and give her the treat.

WAIT: Tells your dog to pause and remain in a general area until you have invited that dog to do the next thing. *Wait* means waiting for the body and mind to pause. Don't move on to anything else until a calm state of mind has occurred. He can stand, sit, or lie down, he just needs to be calm and wait until invited to the next thing.

DOWN: Tells your dog to lie down. She should stay in that spot until you invite her out of it. Trust me when I tell you, I've truly evolved on how I teach a down. The down is one of the last skills I teach a dog. I am not corrective in tone or pressure at all. And I don't depend on purely luring with a treat. You start teaching down, staying right by your dog. You gradually build distance and duration. *Before* you begin trying to teach your dog a down, you must have a strong leash foundation. Be prepared to hold steady on the pressure (whichever method you use) until the millisecond your pooch melts to the ground, then *immediately* release the pressure. Most dogs will initially present moments of fight, flight, or avoidance, but just stick with it. If she pops up, no problem, merely go back and put her back down—one, two, three times, ten times, whatever it takes. Read and look at the enclosed sequence of the three steps to achieve a solid down. Do not move on to the next step until your dog is happily, willingly accepting the position.

DOWN STEP 1: We are using a method described in *The Koehler Method of Dog Training* by William Koehler. My summary goes like this: Put your dog into a sit on your left side. Kneel down on your left knee. Your left hand grasps the running part of your collar securely (so that if a dog spins or whirls, your fingers won't get caught), but don't choke or hurt the dog with your grip. Then apply gentle pressure with your left arm, as much as required, on your dog's back and assist him down while simultaneously moving his front feet forward out from under him with your right arm in a gentle, sweeping motion. Release all pressure the millisecond your dog melts to the ground and quietly, slowly, and gently stroke down his back between his shoulder blades for twenty or so strokes. Then calmly release your dog from the down by inviting him forward. Remember, do not move forward to Step 2 until your dog is calm, accepting, and happy in this position.

DOWN STEP 2: Take the leash in your hand and hold it six to eight inches from the collar. Apply steady and gentle downward pressure at a slight angle—about twenty degrees away from the direction of the dog's body. It's essential that you do not release any pressure at all, holding your hand at the ground until the down is offered. If a dog really gets stuck, you might have progressed too fast. Try taking your free hand and place gentle pressure near the shoulder blades to assist in a downward motion. If a dog quickly yields to the pressure, good. Keep practicing. Note that a very short dog will require you to place your hands closer to the collar or your knuckles will graze the ground with no pressure applied to dog. The millisecond your dog melts into the down, release all pressure and quietly and gently stroke his back from his shoulder blades down his back for about twenty strokes. Then calmly release your dog from the down by inviting him forward. I repeat, do not move forward to Step 3 until your dog is calm, accepting, and happy in this position.

DOWN STEP 3: This step is very similar to Step 2 with the difference being that your foot is used to apply pressure to the leash at the position where your hand would have gone. First, put your dog in a sit. Remain standing upright and use your foot to apply the pressure on the leash about twelve inches from the collar at a slight angle, with the leash going in a direction away from the dog's body. Begin applying gentle, steady, downward pressure with your foot on the leash. The millisecond the dog melts into the down, release all pressure. Quietly and gently stroke his back from his shoulder blades down for about twenty strokes, then calmly release your dog from the down by inviting him forward.

LET'S GO: Tells your dog that you want her to walk with you somewhere. It's distinctly different than a formal heel with military precision. It is a more informal walk, however, your dog needs to remain on either side you desire and come and sit close to you at your side when you stop. He is not required to stay in a glued sit once you stop. Relax your arms and start walking with your natural arm position, gently swinging your arms. You can use this with long-line and dragline work, as well as short-leash walking.

COME: Tells your dog to come to you, finishing with an automatic sit. People always want to know how to make a dog come when called, and one of the things I have found that works great is to play games to get a dog excited to come to me. I love tying a toy to the end of a horse's lunge line and swinging that toy all around for the dog to chase. I allow the dog to "catch" it, then I ask him to come and trade the toy for a treat after he sits in front of me! The dog has fun at every part of the game. I've worked lots of skills in with this one fun game—get it, bring it, come, and leave it are all skills dogs can learn while having a ball! I have a dragline on a dog when I'm working this concept via play so that I'm able to guide, mentor, assist, and otherwise make clear my intent that a dog will be coming to me when I ask him to. I am *always* positive, never corrective. I *always* use an encouraging tone. I *always* mean what I say, the first time. And it's *always* a party once a dog arrives to me. The best parties always have great food, smiles, and are so much fun that you never want to leave and you always want the party to happen again. *Always*. There are additional great games to teach a solid recall in your dog, such as the Paper Plate Recall game created by Dick Russell and the Come When Called game by Wendy and Jack Volhard (see the Reference list at the back of this book for more information).

OFF: Tells your dog to keep her paws off of someone or something, whether it's off you, off the counter, or off the furniture. "Off" means all four feet are on the ground. Teach your dog the "off" command when she is not excited and doesn't particularly want to jump up. Say "up" and encourage the dog to jump up on you. When she jumps up, say "good up!" and praise your dog. Then hook your thumb through your dog's collar and assist her off. Put your dog in a sit and reward! Another variation of this is when your dog has her paws or her body up on something (such as a counter or table), you say "good up" and use a treat in front of her nose to lure her off of the item. As soon as all paws are back on the ground, mark the behavior with a "yes" and give her the treat. Repeat the next four times she gets up on something, then test your cue: Say "off" and see if she gets off. If she does, move on to advance the difficulty. If she does not, then repeat a few more times. If the dog won't follow the treat as you try to lure her off, you need a higher-value treat. And don't forget, your dog always has a leash on so that you can gently use it to reinforce the action. It's important to use a treat or food item that your dog really likes so that getting off of the thing she is on is much more rewarding than staying on it. Now it's time to advance your level of difficulty and "proof" your work. As soon as she gets off of the item when you say "off," mark and treat. Once she is reliably getting off when you cue her, you can start fading the treat part by starting to praise her or by giving her treats randomly.

LEAVE IT: Tells your dog to keep his mouth off of someone or something. I'm a big believer in playing games to teach our dogs while we are having fun. I choose times to teach these skills when the dog has had a bit of exercise and is ready to focus a bit. Show your dog a treat, put it on the floor, and cover it with your hand. When his attention is on your hand or when he tries to get to the treat, say "leave it." Wait for *any* break in attention, then praise your dog and remove your hand, allowing him to get the treat with a "good dog!" Repeat. Keep it light and fun. Increase difficulty by covering the treat with just your index finger. Again, tell him to "leave it" when there is a polite pause and immediately release the treat with praise. Then try placing the treat between your index and middle finger. When your dog reliably ignores the treat on command, place the treat one inch in front of your hand. Here you need to be watchful: He may be faster at getting to the treat than you can cover it. If he does, no harm done, just try again and be a little more watchful.

PAWS UP: Tells your dog to put his front paws up (on whatever you are asking for) in a respectful way, upon your invitation. You can teach "paws up" on a chair, stool, your lap, on your arm, or any other stable, non-slippery, low, secure object. Lure your dog onto the object with a great treat. Keep your hand on his leash close to his collar so that you can control his ascent in the event he wants to jump all the way up. The instant his front two feet come up on the object, mark with a "yes" and treat! Don't *force* the dog to remain. You will gradually grow the duration of "paws up" by holding a treat in front of his nose and releasing the treat when he holds the position for longer periods of time. As with all things, gradually fade the treat as you proof the skill and randomize the delivery of treats.

PLACE: Tells your dog to remain in a comfortable, designated space with a defined boundary until invited off. If your dog gets off place, try to get him back on place without using your hands. Stop his forward motion by standing in front of him. Keep applying physical pressure by moving toward him until he gets all four paws on place. The goal is for the dog to remain on place until you release him off. Over time your ultimate goal is for him to remain on place and choose to relax and be calm. This is a process that takes time. You begin with short time intervals and in a low-distraction environment. Over time you increase the duration and distractions. You grow a dog's ability to tap into a relaxed and calm state of mind gradually. Place is never punishment. It is not a place for toys. He can stand, sit, or lie down, as he chooses. He just can't get off until he's calm and invited by you.

*Nuisance Behaviors*

For nuisance behaviors, you'll find that structure, schedule, and purpose-driven activities fix, reduce, and manage most of them. If your dog begins getting generally naughty or destructive or develops separation anxiety, it could be a symptom of boredom and frustration from a life either spent alone or with too much unearned affection and freedom. The first thing to do is get a leash back on your dog and shut down the silliness by quickly circling your dog around in a counter-clockwise motion to your left side and making him sit. Then you relax and wait for a calm moment before you get moving together. Repeat as often as necessary. Reward and praise only when you've received a calm choice. Also, when your dog is out with you, reduce the time spent on affection and increase time spent on owner-initiated polite exercises, such as a bike ride, a jog, or a brisk walk with your dog. More tethering is always beneficial and essential at this point. And don't forget, every activity does need to be polite and on leash. When you are done, appropriate confinement in a crate after the activity will help to reset your dog's attitude. Nuisance behaviors are indicators of bigger issues, so you'll need to work through the program first before trying different approaches.

# THE WHOLE DOG

We care about the mind, body, and soul of our dogs. If our dogs aren't feeling right, they can't possibly act right. We encourage an approach that considers quality vet care, proper skin care, and a healthy diet. Never underestimate the effect that pain and discomfort can have on the behavior of a dog.

*Vet Care*

A healthy dog is more likely to be a happy dog, and we count on our medical care providers to help us with our dog's overall health. Proper and necessary vaccinations, parasite control, spaying and neutering, chiropractic care, dental care, and eye care are all necessary parts of responsible dog ownership. Always speak to your vet about any concerns you may have about your dog. And finally, educate yourself on proper dog care and problems by asking questions and finding answers from reliable, trusted experts. Be open to more holistic options whenever possible and under the advice of holistic vet professionals.

*Grooming*

Daily grooming is a necessity, and it doesn't have to break the bank. Keeping your pet well groomed does not require going to the salon. Invest in some basic tools appropriate to your dog's coat type and brush your dog daily. When it's bathing time for you pooch, you can wash your dog in your shower with you; it not only makes for a clean-smelling companion, it also helps keep your dog more comfortable while being handled and allows you to spot health problems before they become serious or even life-threatening.

How important is grooming to your pet's comfort and health? Have you ever had your hair in a ponytail that was just a little too tight? Maybe your hair was just bunched up or stuck together? A mat can feel the same way to your dog—a constant pull on the skin. Try to imagine those all over your body, and you have an idea how uncomfortable an ungroomed coat can be.

Your dog doesn't need to know what a mat feels like if you keep him brushed and combed, but that's just the start of the health benefits. Hair has a number of helpful functions, such as regulating a dog's body temperature, protecting from weather fluctuations, and providing protection from the sun and pollutants that would harm your dog's skin, which is seven times more absorptive than a human's.

Different coat types have different needs. Short-coated dogs need more oil in their coats, and most require natural oil additives to assist with moisturization. Medium-coated dogs require more proteins and minerals to keep their skin and hair healthy. Long-haired dogs need extra collagen in their skin and hair. We like misting conditioners for long-haired dogs to help with tangles and mats. Always shampoo and condition with quality products and use brushes and combs made for your dog's particular coat type. Regular grooming allows you to look for lumps, bumps, and injuries, all while clearing mats and ticks from your pooch's coat. Follow up with your veterinarian on any questionable masses you find, and you may detect cancer early enough to save your pet's life.

*Nutrition*

Here's the deal…what we put into our bodies matters. Dogs are carnivores and thrive on a meat-based diet. They have a short and acidic digestive tract. They have sharp teeth with jaws that move vertically. Dogs don't have a carbohydrate-digesting enzyme in their saliva. Foods that convert to sugars are simply not healthy and can contribute to a dog's overly spun-out state of mind. Not all foods are created equal. Ingredients don't lie but can be misleading, so read your labels. You can go to dogfoodadvisor.com to see a rating of your current food. I also recommend the Whole Dog Journal's annual review of foods in the different major food categories of kibble, canned, and raw. The recommended food listed is comprised of foods that have been evaluated in 2017 and as such, is subject to change.

What food is best for your dog? Get educated. Read labels. And don't be afraid to change. Budget realities can also factor in, but realize that if you feed a commercial kibble product, you should also be adding a digestive enzyme to aid in digestion and a probiotic as well. By the time you add in the things you need when eating a kibble product, it can be a push in cost with a high-quality premade raw diet.

*Food Recommendations*

Grain-free commercial kibble
Fromm
Acana
Avoderm
All can be ordered online from PetFlow.com, Amazon.com, or Chewy.com—free shipping available. These are very high quality, but rather expensive kibbles.

Recommended digestive enzymes and probiotics
Endurance supplement from Volhard.com
Nutra Vet supplement
Probios probiotic
Tummy Tunic digestive enzyme from Volhard.com
Optigest digestive enzyme

Soft canned food

Avoderm
Fromm

<u>Freeze-dried raw</u>
Sojo's
Primal
Stella's
Volhard Natural Diet Foundation 2 (you add your raw protein source). Order from Volhard.com

My personal dogs eat a raw diet composed of a "porridge" (it kind of looks like oatmeal) of vegetables, herbs, etc. that I order from Volhard.com (the Natural Diet Foundation 2). I add water and raw meat to it in the ratio outlined on the bag for the weight of the dog. I value and respect Wendy Volhard, who has been talking about raw diet and the health of our dogs for the past thirty-five plus years. I encourage you to read her book, *The Holistic Guide for a Healthy Dog*.

<u>Bones and Treats</u>
Never give your pup or dog chocolate. It contains theobromine, a chemical that is toxic to dogs. Also, don't feed your dog bones that can splinter or that have sharp edges. Large, hard bones such as knuckle and marrow bones are fine, but parboil them to destroy harmful parasites and take them away from your dog if he starts to actually eat the bone rather than just chew on it. There are other ways to satisfy a dog's craving to chew. Commercially available **chew toys** and simulated bones are made for dogs of all sizes. Keep the treats to a minimum and use string cheese or green beans. You don't want to ruin your dog's appetite for eating balanced foods with too many treats!

***PUPPY PIT STOP:*** Feeding Your Puppy: A First-Year Timeline recommendations from the AKC:

Get a high quality food that is specially formulated for puppies! Puppies have different nutritional needs than dogs and require the additional calories and essential nutrients. There are differences between the nutritional needs of small- and large-breed pups as well.

Small-breed pups—those that will weigh 20 lbs. or less when full-grown—grow quickly and reach adulthood by nine months. Large-breed pups—those that will weigh 21 lbs. or more when full-grown—grow more slowly and reach adulthood from fifteen to twenty-four months (Mansourian).

- **6–12 weeks:** Four feedings a day are usually adequate to meet nutritional demands.
- **3–6 months:** Sometime during this period, decrease feedings from four to three a day. A pup should be losing her potbelly and pudginess by twelve weeks. If she is still roly-poly at this age, continue to feed puppy-size portions until body type matures.
- **6–12 months:** Begin feeding twice daily. Spaying or neutering lowers energy requirements slightly; after the procedure, switch from nutrient-rich puppy food to adult maintenance food. Small breeds can make the switch at seven to nine months; bigger breeds at twelve, thirteen, even fourteen months. Err on the side of caution: better to be on puppy food a little too long than not long enough.
- **After 1 year:** Most owners feed adult dogs two half-portions a day.

## CONCLUSION

All of these strategies outlined in this practical guide heavily depend upon the human's involvement and commitment. Dogs are not robots. They are living, breathing creatures with unique personalities. Working with an animal is never a "one and done" deal. It is a lifelong approach that requires continual effort and education. We encourage our clients who work with us at APBC to participate in our ongoing support programs, such as our online community groups, online videos, live streaming, and virtual classes, as well as our on-site pack walks, beneficial socialization, and tune-ups for all our graduates. It is my passion that people and dogs learn to live life together in a safe, sane, and civilized way! Now go on…go live life with your dog!

# ACKNOWLEDGMENTS

I am so grateful for everything in my life, but I would like to send a special "thank you" to those who have helped me in this process of living my passion: my husband, Grant; my daughter, Nicole; my son, Luke; my sister, mom, and dad; my mentors in both the horse and dog world; my entire team at APBC; and my dogs, who shaped my past, my present, and my future. When it comes to this book, I want to thank my editor, Jennifer Westbrook, my marketing coordinator, Lacey Akins, and my son, Luke Rodges, all who have helped me weave my way through this technical world of book design and production.

# REFERENCES

American Veterinary Society of Animal Behavior. *Puppy Socialization Position Statement.* AVSABonline.com, 2008.

Koehler, William. *The Koehler Method of Dog Training.* New York: Howell Book House, 1981.

Mansourian, Erika. "Puppy Feeding Fundamentals." American Kennel Club, June 15, 2016, http://www.akc.org/content/health/articles/puppy-feeding-fundamentals.

*Oxford Living Dictionaries*, s.v. "accept," accessed September 10, 2017, https://en.oxforddictionaries.com/definition/accept.

Russell, Dick. "Paper Plate Recalls: Teaching dogs to come by teaching them to run away." *Safe Hands Journal* 5, no. 1 (2004): 10-12.

Thompson, Bev. "Why Tone of Voice Matters When Training Your Dog." Anything Pawsable, accessed September 10, 2017, http://www.anythingpawsable.com/why-tone-of-voice-matters-when-training-your-dog.

*Vocabulary.com Dictionary*, s.v. "rituals," accessed September 10, 2017, https://www.vocabulary.com/dictionary/ritual.

Volhard, Jack and Wendy. "Canine Personality Profile." Volhard.com, accessed September 1, 2017, http://www.volhard.com/pages/canine-personality-profile.php.

———. "Coming When Called." Volhard.com, accessed September 10, 2017, http://www.volhard.com/pages/coming-when-called.php.

Volhard, Wendy. *The Holistic Guide for a Healthy Dog*. New York: Howell Book House, 2000.

# ABOUT THE AUTHOR

Alyson Rodges is a certified dog trainer specializing in puppies. A lifelong animal lover with a lifetime of training experience under her belt, Aly enjoys teaching people the necessary skills for them to better understand, communicate with, and enjoy a balanced life with their dogs. Aly's Puppy Boot Camp, which launched in 2012, is located in Arroyo Grande on the gorgeous Central Coast of California, where Alyson lives with her family (the two and four-legged ones!). You can find out more about Aly and her boot camps at [www.alysonrodges.com](www.alysonrodges.com) or email her at info@alysonrodges.com.

This Pillars of Pack Leadership practical guide has everything you need to go live life with your dog, *but* you might want more.

Well, you can have it! I have recently introduced the…

**Pillars of Pack Leadership® Academy**

The Academy is an online course that will visually guide you through this book. It is full of helpful worksheets, quizzes, and cheat sheets. You even get access to a private Facebook community that you can go to for advice and ideas…I even pop in the group once a week to answer questions personally.

I want to invite you to join our community! Visit my website for more information.

**www.alysonrodges.com**

Made in the USA
San Bernardino, CA
03 June 2020